LEVIS... & HO...

A GUIDE FOR ADVENTURERS

St Mary's Church

North Yorkshire Moors Railway

Norman hunters in the Royal Forest of Pickering

Saltergate smugglers

Introducing Levisham Estate – over three thousand acres of spellbinding scenery in the heart of the North York Moors, kept by the National Park Authority on behalf of the nation.

WELCOME TO LEVISHAM ESTATE!

Levisham Estate is virtually the North York Moors in miniature. Into 3,358 acres it packs almost everything that gives the National Park its unique character: spectacular landforms, ancient woodlands, world-class archaeology, romantic ruins, teeming wildlife, and of course, mile after mile of our famous heather moorland.

Some of the best-loved beauty spots in the National Park are part of the estate. The majestic scenery of the Hole of Horcum, a vast natural amphitheatre, has been stopping travellers in their tracks for centuries. Newtondale, with its celebrated steam railway, is a place of pilgrimage not just for steam enthusiasts but for geologists, photographers, naturalists, ramblers and people who simply know a beautiful view when they see one.

Away from the famous landmarks, though, people are few and far between. Step off the beaten track and you'll begin to discover the area's lesser-known treasures. Because almost all of the estate is Open Access Land, you're free to walk, run, climb, picnic and take pictures pretty much wherever you like. The wild expanses of Fen Moor, the rich wetlands of Nab Farm and the archaeological wonders of Levisham Moor are yours to explore.

Levisham Estate is owned and cared for by the North York Moors National Park Authority on behalf of the nation. The Authority bought Levisham Moor and the Hole of Horcum in 1976 when the character of the landscape was under threat from intensive agriculture and forestry. Fen Moor, Nab Farm and Levisham Woods were added to the estate in the 1980s. In the years since then the Authority has worked with local farmers to ensure that this special area is conserved for future generations to enjoy.

About this guide
The aim of this guide is to help you get the most out of your visit to Levisham Estate. It doesn't try to tell you everything there is to know about the area – that would take much more than a short booklet. Instead we've had a go at anticipating some of the questions that might pop into your head as you're exploring. What are those humps and bumps in the heather? How did that valley get to be such an odd shape? How old are these woods? Did someone once live in that tumbledown tower?

By far the best way to get to know Levisham Estate is to walk it. On pages 11, 23 and 31 of this booklet you'll find examples of walking routes, each of which links together places and features of interest. If you want to try any of the routes out, you'll need a decent pair of boots, and a set of waterproofs is always a good idea.

Remember that the mist can roll in without much warning, so unless you're confident with a map and compass, it might be best to give the moors a miss in bad weather. The map you need for walking on the estate is Ordnance Survey OL27 North York Moors Eastern Area.

Read this booklet however you like – cover to cover, back to front, on the hoof, in the bath, in any old order. We hope it will inspire you to set off on many future Levisham and Horcum adventures. Happy explorations!

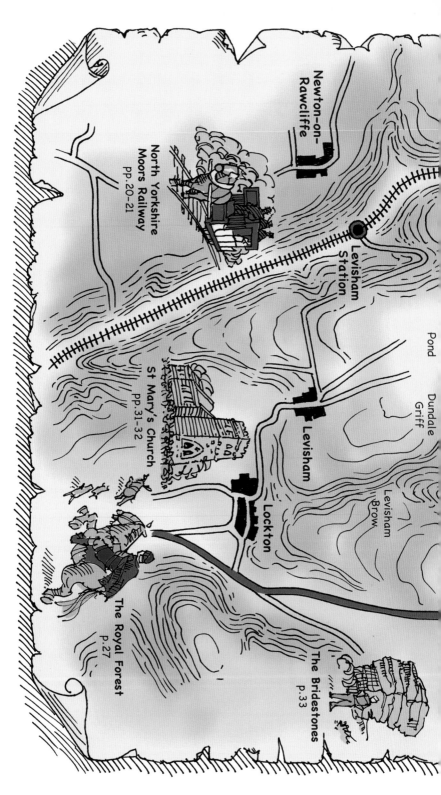

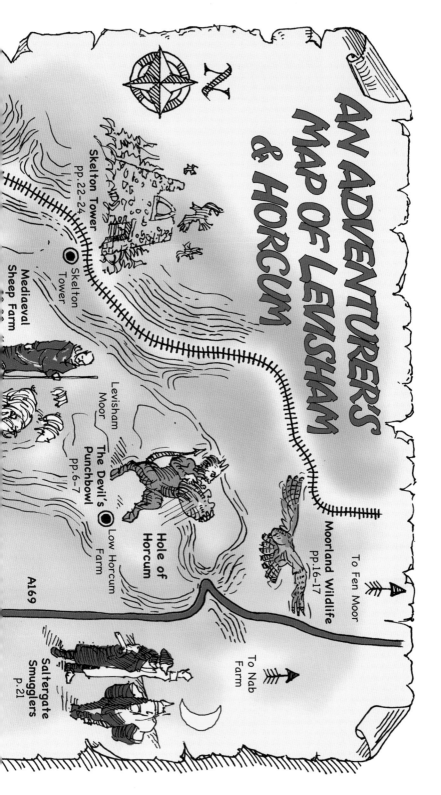

THE DEVIL'S PUNCHBOWL

The Hole of Horcum is one of the great spectacles of the North York Moors: a huge natural amphitheatre, 400 feet deep and more than half a mile across, scooped out of the moor by thousands of years of spring-water erosion.

'The Devil's Punchbowl' is its local name. It has an old association with the Devil, perhaps on account of the gallows that once stood upon its rim near Saltergate, or the vapours boiling from its gloomy depths when the moors are in fog.

According to legend, the Devil himself created the Hole. The story goes like this. An old witch had sold her soul to him in return for magical powers. When he came to collect, she refused to surrender her soul and fled across the moor with the Devil hot on her heels.

Unable to catch up, he flew into a rage and gouged out a huge handful of earth to throw at her. It missed and landed a mile away to form Blakey Topping.

Mark Denton

You can still see the Devil's fingermarks in the hillside on the far side of the Hole from the road. Horcum hokum or the Hole truth? – see for yourself!

How the Hole was made

The rocks that once filled the Hole have been eaten away grain by grain in a process called spring-sapping. Running water bubbling from the hillside has gradually undermined the slopes above, flushing loose material away downstream. Over thousands of years a narrow valley has been widened and deepened into an enormous empty cauldron.

This process is still going on. The Hole is still growing. Eventually it will breach Horcum Dike, swallow the Whitby-Pickering road, gulp down Saltergate car park, and continue on its creeping course across the moor.

AN ICE AGE RELIC – THE DWARF CORNEL

The Hole of Horcum is the most southerly place in Britain that this lovely rare flower is found. It's usually found in much colder conditions, yet it has survived out of its natural temperature range for 10,000 years. Now time may be running out for this tough little plant: if climate change makes the North York Moors warmer and drier, the dwarf cornel could disappear from Yorkshire forever.

A WINTER'S TALE

One wild winter night in the late 1960s a Hole way of life came to an end. A single ferocious snowstorm signalled the demise of a century and a half of farming tradition in the Hole of Horcum.

Up to then there were two farmsteads in the valley. Low Horcum Farm was built in 1811. Little now remains but the farmhouse, which lies next to the footpath from Saltergate. High Horcum Farm was built at around the same time and lay slightly further to the northeast.

Life in the Hole had its share of hardships. Neither farm had electricity or running water. You can still see the outside privy at Low Horcum. Visiting it must have been an uncomfortable experience in the

Jack Mackley of High Horcum Farm, with his dogs Lassie and Gypsy, in around 1950.

Photo: Sidney Smith. Obtainable from Beck Isle Museum, Pickering

Low Horcum Farm, photographed before it fell to ruin. High Horcum can be seen in the background.

cold months of the year. The valley floor has an average altitude of 525 feet (160m) above sea-level and the bare moors above offer no shelter from the wind.

Avalanche!

That fateful winter night, the north wind swept over the moors, bringing heavy snow. It gathered on the lip of the Hole of Horcum, forming an overhanging ledge, or cornice. At last it collapsed under its own weight and plummeted down the hillside onto High Horcum Farm.

The crash as the avalanche laid waste to High Horcum was heard at the other farm half a mile away. What was left of the building couldn't be saved and had to be demolished.

Low Horcum itself only survived a few more years. During the bitterly cold winter of 1982-3, some roofing work was left unfinished by the farm's tenant and the weather crept in. By springtime the buildings were so dilapidated they had become dangerous. The North York Moors National Park Authority, which by then owned the farm as part of Levisham Estate, had no choice other than to demolish the barns. The solitary farmhouse was made safe and now stands as a monument to a bygone age.

9

THE ENCHANTED WORLD OF THE GRIFF

Some of the Devil's fingermarks on the side of the Hole of Horcum are actually deep rocky ravines known as griffs. They've been etched into the sandstone by water running off Levisham Moor, and may carry fierce torrents after a lot of rain or snow. But more often than not they're dry.

Standing in the mouth of the griff and peering into its shady depths is like looking into a fairytale kingdom. Ancient oaks clutch at the steep sides with fabulously gnarled roots. A velvet mantle of moss covers rocks and branches. Pebbles spun by eddies in the current have scoured out little cup-shaped golden hollows in the sandstone, where they collect like spent coins. Ferns sprout from damp crevices, and wood sorrel and herb Robert flourish at your feet.

You step back into the light and the spell is broken. Have you been away for a few minutes or a hundred years?

Message to adventurers
Griffs are very sensitive to disturbance. They can also be dangerous, with slippery surfaces and falling rocks. Please look from the path rather than walking in the griff itself – there are some ideal viewpoints on the public footpath alongside Dundale Griff.

A HOLE OF HORCUM ADVENTURE

Take a sip at the Devil's Punchbowl with this wonderfully scenic walk. The route leads you down into the Hole of Horcum, past the lonesome remains of Low Horcum Farm. There's a chance to peer into magical, moss-clad Dundale Griff. The last section is the perfect introduction to Levisham Moor, one of the most remarkable historic landscapes in Britain.

Start: Saltergate car park
(map ref: SE 853 937)
Time: 2–3 hours
Length: 5 miles
Terrain: on good paths with a couple of short climbs. Can be muddy in places.

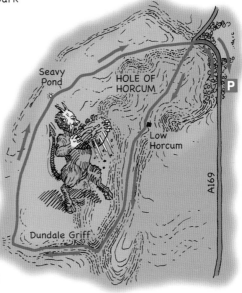

1. Cross the road at one of the crossing points and turn right, following the path around the edge of the Hole of Horcum towards the hairpin bend.
2. Turn left before the moor gate and follow the path steeply down into the Hole.
3. Cross the stream and keep going, passing to the right of Low Horcum Farm. Where the path splits in two just after the farmhouse, take the lower righthand path through the middle of the field. Stick to this path, ignoring any turnings off to the left.
4. Cross two streams and turn right, following the footpath signposted to Dundale Pond.
5. At Dundale Pond turn right up the slope on the bridleway signposted to Saltergate.
6. Continue along the bridleway past Seavy Pond, across the moor and back towards the main road.
7. Follow the path back up to the car park.

HOW THE MOORS CAME TO BE

To understand how the moors came to be, we need to go back in time to 8,000 years ago and picture this bare landscape covered in ... what, heather? Bracken? Snow? No: trees.

For thousands of years after the last ice age, Levisham Moor was covered in oakwoods with grassy clearings where red deer and wild cattle grazed.

The first people (c.8000–6000 BC) hunted the grazing animals and gathered the fruits of the forest.

To attract more grazing animals the hunters probably cleared small areas of trees.

About 4,000 years ago, farming came to the region. The population grew. Now larger areas of trees were cleared to make way for fields.

This was slash-and-burn-style agriculture: when the fields were exhausted, the farmers cleared more forest to plant their crops.

The abandoned fields were given over to sheep. Their constant grazing stopped the natural woodlands from growing back.

Without the trees to protect the thin soils the rain washed more nutrients away.

In the Iron Age larger and larger areas of woodland were cleared. At the same time the climate became cooler and wetter.

The soils got poorer and poorer until they would no longer support crops. Only hardy plants like heather and coarse grasses would grow.

By Roman times the transformation of the landscape was complete. The moors as we know them had come to be.

HUMPS AND BUMPS AND STONES AND BONES

Q. What's the largest ancient monument in the North York Moors? (You might be thinking of historic houses or ruined abbeys or even old industrial sites. If so, the answer will surprise you ...)
A. Levisham Moor.

Over 500 acres of Levisham Moor are protected by law as a Scheduled Monument, making it one of the largest, if not the largest, in the whole country. Dotted all over the moor, half-hidden in the heather, are traces of human occupation. Together they tell a story that stretches back 4,000 years to the early Bronze Age.

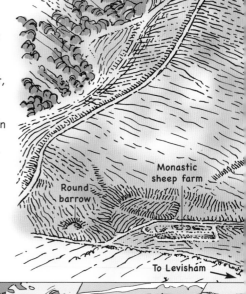

Monastic sheep farm

Round barrow

To Levisham

Before 4000 BC Mesolithic people use this area for hunting and gathering

2000 BC The first farmers settle in the area and clear land for cultivation

2000–1500 BC Bronze Age settlers bury their dead in round barrows

1000–400 BC Late Bronze Age and early Iron Age people build boundary dykes

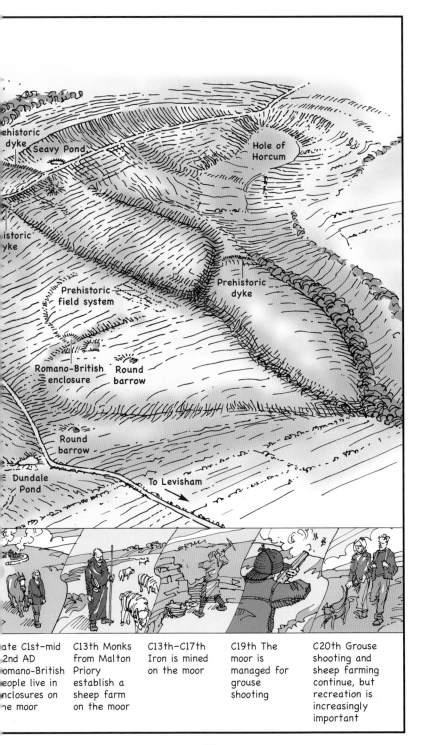

Prehistoric dyke

Seavy Pond

Hole of Horcum

Prehistoric dyke

Prehistoric field system

Prehistoric dyke

Romano-British enclosure

Round barrow

Round barrow

Dundale Pond

To Levisham

ate C1st–mid 2nd AD omano-British eople live in nclosures on he moor

C13th Monks from Malton Priory establish a sheep farm on the moor

C13th–C17th Iron is mined on the moor

C19th The moor is managed for grouse shooting

C20th Grouse shooting and sheep farming continue, but recreation is increasingly important

15

MOORLAND WILDLIFE

What's that hiding in the heather? The chances are it's one of the birds and beasties below ...

Stoat

Wheatear

NEWTONDALE

Pickering Beck meanders along the bottom of Newtondale. Can this lazy stream really have carved such a spectacular valley?

Imagine a river flowing through a 250-foot-deep gorge. The source of this mighty torrent is an immense cold dark lake, its east and west shores lapping against towering cliffs of ice. You're picturing Newtondale at the height of the last ice age.

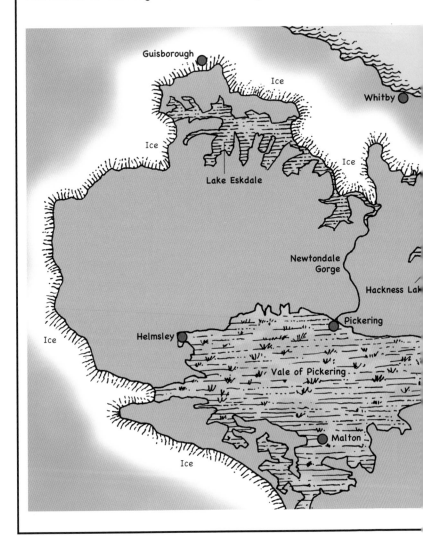

Newtondale

The lake lay in what is now Eskdale. It was 20 miles long, several miles wide, and dammed at either end by the ice sheets. The moors to the south were a bare frozen plateau, lashed by arctic winds. Beyond them lay a region of fog-shrouded marshland and standing water, filling today's Vale of Pickering.

So the landscape remained for millennia. Then, about 20,000 years ago, something changed. The weather eroded part of the surface of the moorland plateau to below the water level of Lake Eskdale. The lake began to overflow.

Slowly but relentlessly, a colossal volume of water bulldozed a trench 12 miles long through the moorland plateau. Eventually it burst out the other side, spewing rock into the Vale of Pickering.

And as the waters subsided, they revealed their parting gift: Newtondale, our own miniature Grand Canyon, the finest example of a glacial-lake overflow channel in England.

Scarborough

Ice

Filey

Ice

Bridlington

GENTLEMEN AND PIONEERS

Travellers in olden times tended to give Newtondale a wide berth. Who knew what was lurking in its marshy, overgrown depths? For the people of Lockton and Levisham, the mighty gorge to the west was always a mixed blessing; it acted as a natural barrier, keeping the world from their doors. But with the dawn of the modern age, all that was to change.

A spirit of improvement

In 1793 a committee of eighteen local gentlemen began drumming up support for a Whitby-Pickering canal. It was to occupy an obvious natural corridor through the moors: Newtondale.

Grain, timber and stone from Pickering would go up the canal to Whitby. Lime, salt and fish would come back down. The cost of building the canal was estimated at £66,447, nearly £4 million in today's money. Investors could expect a 5% return. Among the committee members rubbing their hands at the prospect of a tidy profit was Robert Skelton, rector of Levisham from 1786 to 1818.

Making tracks

Enthusiasm for the canal must have ebbed away, because the scheme never went ahead. But the committee's vision of Newtondale as a bustling corridor for trade lived on. When the railway pioneer George Stephenson was asked to look at potential routes for a Whitby-Pickering railway line, he plumped for the course through Newtondale that had been chosen for the canal.

GEORGE STEPHENSON

This time the vision came to life. The railway line opened in 1836. In the beginning the coaches were pulled by horses. But in 1847 the line was extended to York and the horses gave way to steam engines. Trains puffed back and forth through the moors until 1965, when commercial services on the line ended.

Part of the line was reopened a few years later as a heritage railway. The North Yorkshire Moors Railway, as it's known, is a great way of getting to and from Levisham Estate. Why not combine a trip on the train with a walk? Try the one on pages 23–24 if you're stuck for ideas.

Smuggler's highway

Before the railway, the main route across the moors to the coast was a rough track that ran northeast from Saltergate to Lilla Cross and on to Whitby. Originally intended for carrying salt and fish inland – hence the name 'Saltergate' – it soon became notorious as a smuggler's route.

In the 1760s investors began raising funds to lay a brand new turnpike, or toll road, right over the top of the moor. Built entirely from scratch, it was specially designed to carry wheeled traffic. By the 1780s the road was complete and stagecoaches were plying between Whitby and Pickering. Today it goes by the poetic name of the A169.

THE LODGER ON CORNHILL POINT

If you've ever ridden the railway through Newtondale, you may have seen the gaunt silhouette of a building on the skyline where the steam train slows on the bend under Corn Hill Point. This enigmatic ruin commands one of the finest views in the National Park. But what was it? Who lived there?

The building is known as Skelton Tower after the man who built it: the second Reverend Robert Skelton, rector of Levisham from 1819 to 1877 and son of the Robert Skelton whom we encountered on page 20, rubbing his hands and dreaming of canals. The tower dates from around 1830. Skelton Jr was a keen sportsman, and he used it as overnight lodgings after a day's shooting on the moor.

Thanks to the building's solitary position, picturesque setting and fanciful design, it's easy to imagine Skelton coming here to mope and commune with nature in the fashionable Romantic style. Perhaps the view gave him inspiration for his sermons. Or perhaps it simply saved him the trouble of slogging back up the hill to the rectory.

This grassy headland is called Corn Hill Point, by the way, because the pastures around about were ploughed up and used for growing crops during the Napoleonic wars.

As you can see from this old photo, Skelton Tower was once much grander than it is today. It's long been a popular spot with walkers and daytrippers. The hat and boots lying on the ground to the right of the tower in the photo belong to a party of picnickers who are admiring the view just out of shot.

A SKELTON TOWER ADVENTURE

This short outing starts with a train journey back in time. Get aboard the North Yorkshire Moors Railway in 21st-century Pickering and alight at Levisham Station in Edwardian times. From here it's on foot. The walk to Skelton Tower takes you along the lush floor of Newtondale and up onto the heather-scented terraces of Corn Hill Point for a view you'll never forget.

Start: Levisham Station (map ref: SE 818 911). Limited parking.
Time: 2 hours
Length: 3.5 miles
Terrain: Generally good paths. A steep climb near the start, but then mainly flat with a gentle downhill stretch at the end.

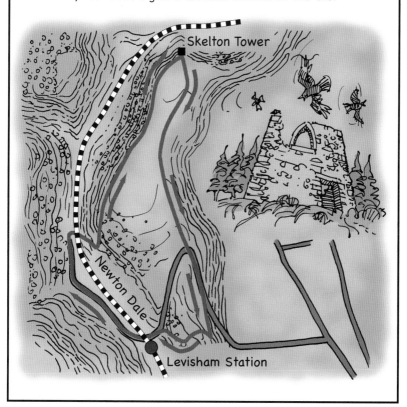

Skelton Tower fell into disrepair after Robert Skelton's death. By the 1970s the whole building was in danger of collapse. In 1978 the tower was partly restored and made safe by the North York Moors National Park Authority to commemorate the first 25 years of the National Park (1952–77).

1. Cross the railway by the signal box and follow the forest road round to the right.

2. After about a mile turn right on a footpath signposted to Newtondale Halt (via moors).

3. Cross Pickering Beck via a footbridge, then cross the railway track. Don't forget to watch out for trains!

4. Follow the waymarkers up a steep path flanking the edge of a plantation.

5. The path strikes away to the left. At the top of the hill you'll reach a plateau of open moorland and rough pasture. Pick up a faint path skirting the edge of the plateau – Skelton Tower will appear in the distance.

6. Enjoy the view at the tower, then face away from Newtondale and look for two clear paths. Take the one on the right, which will bring you to a wide grassy track. Follow this track to join the road at a sharp bend.

7. Walk up the road, then take the bridleway off to the right, keeping to the grassy upper path.

8. Continue straight ahead beside the fence until you reach a field gate and stile on your right.

9. The path goes along the top of the field, then down to a gate at the bottom right. Head downhill through woodland to the road, and turn left to return to Levisham Station.

INTO THE GREENWOOD

If you look at the map of Levisham Estate inside the front cover of this booklet, you'll see that the southern part of it consists of two long, thin tentacles of green that curl protectively around Levisham village and its surrounding fields.

Strike out in this direction and you'll find yourself in an altogether different countryside from the moorlands to the north – fresh pastures, shady conifer forests, and beautiful emerald-green broadleaved woodland, laced with ancient trackways and ringing with birdsong.

These woods, clothing the steep valley sides that the plough couldn't reach, are hundreds, maybe even thousands of years old. They can't be said to be wholly natural, though, because of their long history of human exploitation.

For centuries local people practised coppicing here – cutting

Levisham Wood

individual trees back to a stump and then harvesting the regrowth for fuel and building materials. Examples of coppiced trees, now disused and left to mature, can still be seen in the woods around Levisham. Look out for several trunks sprouting from the same broad stump, known as a 'stool'.

Alien invaders!

The woods around Levisham and Horcum are mostly made up of oak and birch or ash. These are native trees - they were among the species that colonised Britain after the last ice age. Here and there, though, you'll spot some more recent intruders ...

Conifers like western hemlock (from North America) were planted in the 1960s to provide a fast-growing source of timber. They're bad news for wildlife because they shade out other greenery, so they're gradually being removed to make room for more native trees.

Not all alien invaders are unwelcome. Many people think of sycamore as a native, but in fact it was only introduced a few hundred years ago - not long in tree terms. It's made itself quite at home in Levisham Wood, and only needs thinning out occasionally to make sure it doesn't take the place over.

FROM LITTLE ACORNS ...

Take your ease beneath the spreading bough of an oak tree and sooner or later you'll be rewarded with a glimpse of a jay.

This colourful member of the crow family is enormously important to the survival of oakwoods because of its habit of burying stores of acorns. A single jay in the course of a season can plant thousands of them, many of which will grow into seedlings. In a typical autumn Britain's jays together plant as many as one and a half billion acorns!

THE ROYAL FOREST OF PICKERING

The woods around Levisham are remnants of a much larger area of woodland. Domesday Book, the great survey of England compiled after the Norman Conquest, says that in 1086 Pickering possessed an area of woodland '16 leagues in length and four of breadth' – about twenty-four miles by six. It spread across half a dozen parishes, including Levisham.

Under William the Conqueror, this huge acreage of trees became part of the Royal Forest of Pickering. The word 'forest' in this context means a hunting ground, and only part of the Forest of Pickering was wooded – in fact, most of it was moorland. It also included farms, villages and open fields, and was protected by special laws, like a cross between a game reserve and a modern National Park.

Only the rich and powerful had the right to hunt the deer and wild swine that roamed the forest. Poachers and trespassers were punished severely. They could be imprisoned in Pickering Castle and even have their eyes gouged out, their hands chopped off, or their foreheads branded with hot irons.

WOODLAND WILDLIFE

If you go down to the woods today ... keep your eyes peeled for some of the following special critters!

Roe Deer

Nuthatch

Green Woodpecker

Badger

Park Ranger

Fox

MONKS, MOORS AND MUTTON

Hunting was one of two great uses of the uplands in mediaeval times. The other was sheep farming. A few fields away from Levisham village, where Braygate Lane leads out onto the open moor, is a vivid reminder of the heyday of the wool trade – the still-traceable remains of a 13th-century sheep farm.

Wool was the oil of the Middle Ages and the equivalents of the big oil companies were the monasteries. They rose to wealth and power after the Norman Conquest. At their height the monasteries had populations numbering in the hundreds; and so, in spite of their dedication to a life of poverty and simplicity, the monks became hardheaded businessmen and farmers in order to support themselves.

By the 13th century around a third of the North York Moors was under monastic control. Huge areas of land were given over to grazing sheep. The monks tended their flocks from outlying farms called granges. A sheep grange is known as a bercary. A typical moorland bercary had two or three hundred sheep.

The Levisham bercary lay to the west of Dundale Pond, then as now a watering place for sheep. The land was given to the monks of Malton Priory by the lord of the Manor of Levisham, Ralph de Bolebec.

You can still see the outlines of enclosures and the foundations of farm buildings. Stand among the fallen stones in the twilight and it's not hard to peel away the centuries and picture the brother-shepherds moving to and fro in the heather, softly calling in their flocks for the night.

A MEDIAEVAL ADVENTURE

This walk's a beauty. Forest tracks lead you along Levisham Brow and down to a perfect beckside picnic spot. Woodland then gives way to moorland as you head for Dundale Pond and the evocative remains of a mediaeval sheep farm. From there you follow a gentle trail south to the age-old meeting-place of roads known as Farwath. Last on the mediaeval itinerary is the melancholy ruin of 12th-century St Mary's Church.

Start: Levisham village (map ref: SE 833 904). Roadside parking - please park considerately.
Time: 3-4 hours
Length: 6.5 miles
Terrain: Clear paths throughout. One or two steep bits, but mainly easy going. Can be squelchy underfoot after wet weather.

1. Head south out of Levisham village along the main street, as though going to Lockton. Leave the road by a bench at the brow of the hill and take a clear path along the top of the escarpment.

2. After about a mile and a half of pleasant walking with fine views, the path drops down to a grassy streambank. Strike off to the west on a path signposted to Dundale Pond.

3. A stone's throw past the pond are the remains of the medieval bercary, lying either side of the path. Keep going westwards, picking up the line of a drystone wall before commencing a steep descent to the road.

4. Go left and tramp the tarmac for a couple of hundred yards, then take a bridleway off to your right. Keep to this path and you'll eventually arrive at a gateway into the woods.

5. Head downhill through conifer trees and emerge into a field beside the railway. For the next mile the path dips in and out of the wood, leaving it once and for all near Farwath.

6. Head over towards the farm buildings. Pass through a straggly line of trees and across the next field to a footbridge over the beck.

7. Follow the track away from the farm buildings to pick up the old green lane known as Sleights Road. The beck should now be on your left. Head roughly northwards, back into the trees …

8. … and then back out again. Carry on through a series of fields. At length you'll come to a fork in the path. Go left, over another footbridge. St Mary's Church is a short way beyond.

9. Last bit: carry on up the track from the church, bearing right to arrive at the road. Turn left and walk a short distance up the hill before finding a path off to the right through the trees. An invigorating climb later, you'll emerge by a familiar-looking wooden bench. Levisham village is only a brief hobble away.